The Oxford Centre fo

Learning
in Teams

A Tutor Guide

© Oxford Centre for Staff Development 1995

Published by
THE OXFORD CENTRE FOR STAFF DEVELOPMENT
Oxford Brookes University
Gipsy Lane
Headington
Oxford
OX3 0BP

Learning in Teams: A Tutor Guide. ISBN 1 873576 21 8

British Library Cataloguing-in-Publication Data. A catalogue record for this book is available from the British Library.

Designed and Typeset in 10.5 on 14 pt Palatino and Helvetica by Ann Trew

Printed in Great Britain by
Oxonian Rewley Press Ltd
Oxford

Printed on paper produced from sustainable forests.

First Printed 1995
Reprinted 1998

Introduction: Why use teams?

At the start of 1995 it was reported that graduate recruiters in the UK had more jobs on offer than ever before, but that they were very disappointed with the quality of graduates and were not filling all their positions. In particular they were dismayed by the continuing lack of communication and teamwork skills of graduates and their lack of experience of working cooperatively. A similar finding was reported following a survey of employers in Australia in 1994. In jobs people are normally expected to work together in work groups of various kinds, and even university research is undertaken in teams. In contrast most undergraduate education, like most school education, is tackled alone and in competition. The underlying process of higher education is too different from working life to prepare students adequately. The academic/vocational debate has tended to be conceived of in terms of differences in content, but differences in process may be just as important. But while academic and vocational content may be in competition with each other, processes such as learning cooperatively in teams achieve both goals better, improving learning and preparing students for research as well as for jobs.

Over the past five or so years there has been unprecedented attention paid to the development of transferable skills in universities and colleges through the Enterprise in Higher Education Programme and other initiatives. Team project work has been adopted in many courses in many universities – and not just in ex-polytechnics and vocational courses. There has also been imaginative experimentation with a whole range of peer tutoring and other cooperative learning processes. Clearly these efforts have not had the kind of impact which was intended. This seems partly a matter of scale and timing – these methods have not yet been adopted widely enough or long enough to have an overall significance. But it is also likely to be partly a matter of sophistication. Much teamwork has been introduced with little understanding of what is involved. Students have often still been assessed individually and there are few rewards for those who have good teamwork skills.

Where any teamwork training has been introduced this has tended to be based on books and manuals on teamwork in organisations outside higher education. However, student teams are quite unlike management teams. They are hierarchically flat with equal status members rather than having a superior in charge and minions who do the leg work. They tend to have similar knowledge and skills rather than having been put together specifically because their skills are different and complement one another. They may never work in the same team again, whereas in work they may be stuck with the same colleagues for years, and there are none of the "boundary" issues associated with work teams and the organisations they work within. As a result most publications on effective teamwork have little to offer students.

This manual is designed to help tutors to plan the productive use of student teams and to support their operation in ways which are more likely to develop the kinds of team skills which students need, whatever they do after they have finished studying. It also addresses tricky issues such as the assessment of teams, the formation of teams and the design of appropriate tasks and assignments for teams.

Tutors have limited time, resources and, in all probability, skills with which to develop students' team skills. Most of their development is going to have to be undertaken by the students themselves. This guide has been written to complement two publications written for students specifically to enable them to work effectively in teams with minimal outside assistance and to develop and monitor their own team skills.

Learning in Teams: A Student Guide is a 16-page booklet intended as an introduction to teamwork or to support short team tasks. It contains ten key pieces of advice and is designed to be used as an extended handout, to be read and discussed within each team.

Learning in Teams: A Student Manual is a 62-page publication designed to support teams who will be together for a substantial project and who need to be a little more sophisticated about how they organise themselves. It takes the same ten pieces of advice as the *Student Guide* and provides exercises, checklists and explanations which enable teams to develop all aspects of their teamwork quite independently.

These two publications are being purchased in bulk by departments to be used to support all student teams on a course. Characteristically each individual is given a copy of the *Student Guide* and each team a copy of the *Student Manual*. They are sometimes sold to students, sometimes loaned and sometimes given free.

Section 4 of this *Tutor Guide* explores how the *Student Guide* and *Student Manual* can be used to run classroom team development exercises.

1.1 Advantages to tutors

Improved student performance

- Maximum total performance from any group of people is achieved not when individuals compete against one another but when individuals cooperate within groups and the groups compete against one another. Teamwork achieves this.

- Teams can be set tasks which are larger, more complex and sophisticated, which involve more variables or analysing more data, and which are more interesting than tasks that individuals can reasonably tackle.

- The outcomes of teamwork are almost always of a higher standard than those of individuals and very often produce higher average marks and higher top marks. As class sizes increase and it becomes more difficult to provide the support for independent study which students need, it is common for the top end of quality to be lost. Lower level objectives can be achieved but not higher level objectives. Teamwork offers a way of recovering this quality.

- There is relatively little chance of team failure, and much less than that of individual student failure.

4

Improved support for students

- Students are capable of providing a great deal of mutual support for one another.

- Students have more time than tutors, and team members are more likely than tutors to be accessible and available when individuals need help.

- In contexts where, on account of resource problems, tutor-led discussion groups have grown large and infrequent and individual tuition and feedback have been cut back, teamwork can increase the amount and improve the quality of involvement in discussion between students and foster informal peer tutoring and peer feedback.

Improved transferable skills

- Teamwork can involve a wide range of transferable skills, and team projects are an ideal vehicle for building the demand for the use of skills into learning tasks. Team projects can involve leadership, interpersonal skills, negotiation, oral and written communication, time and task management, research and information skills, chairing meetings and almost any other skill you want to build in.

- Teamwork is almost universal in industry and commerce – whether it is software development teams, primary health care teams, management teams or "quality circles". Even academic life is increasingly undertaken in course teams and research teams. The kind of individualistic competitive learning normally entered upon in higher education is a poor preparation for subsequent work. Using teamwork with realistic tasks can bring elements of the outside world into otherwise narrowly academic tasks. Students with extensive experience of cooperative learning are more employable.

Resource savings

- Teams can share resources which individuals might otherwise use: books, articles, equipment, materials, artefacts, fieldwork sites, etc.

- Supervising a team of six may take twice as long as supervising an individual – but not six times as long. Time saved in this way can be partly reinvested in developing team skills so that students are even more independent and need even less supervision in the future.

- Marking the products of teamwork has the potential to save a great deal of time – again involving fewer hours than marking the products of all the individuals involved.

1.2 Advantages – and some disadvantages – to students

Advantages

- Some students find studying alone socially isolating, especially in large classes or on modular courses where there are weak social groupings, and teamwork can be a very welcome opportunity to get to know and study with others.

- Teamwork can provide an excellent opportunity to develop skills. Students preparing a profile for employers relish teamwork and the experience this gives them.

- Teamwork usually involves more interesting tasks than individual study – larger, more complex and more open ended than can be tackled alone. Students often find themselves putting more effort into working with others because it is more engaging.

- Average and weak students have the opportunity to study with others who are more able, and this can be enormously helpful and stimulating. They can see how successful students go about their work as well as gaining informal peer tutoring and peer feedback.

- Teamwork can be less risky than individual work, with a much lower chance of completely ploughing a project and getting very poor marks.

Disadvantages

- There is a possibility of being dragged down by poor or lazy students. A student heading for a first might feel threatened by working with others heading for 2:2s, and such students may find themselves doing a tremendous amount of work to compensate for weaker colleagues. It is possible to avoid this problem through various assessment devices (see Section 2.4 below) so that excellent students need not suffer or worry.

- There may be a loss of individual choice – tackling a topic the tutor has set the group or which the majority in the team have chosen rather than what the individual might have preferred.

- Students working alone undertake every aspect of an assignment themselves and so learn about every angle. In a team they may undertake only one or two components and learn less about the others. If there is a specified syllabus which is assessed through other means, such as an unseen exam which could ask about anything on the syllabus, this can represent a threat. Individuals may bail out of the team in order to revise topics they have not been involved with in the team. Teamwork may be inappropriate in such circumstances.

I have come across courses where students work in teams to such an extent that they beg to be allowed to work alone, and the balance of advantages and disadvantages may shift depending on what else students are currently doing elsewhere on their courses.

Setting up and assessing teamwork

There are several types of team in which students learn. Project teams are task-oriented: the main goal is the completion of the task. This *Tutor Guide* is primarily about such task-oriented project teams. In contrast, learning teams are process-oriented, and the focus is on mutual support and learning to learn rather than on completing tasks. The students within learning teams may not even be on the same course and they may have no common study tasks to undertake. Section 2.7 is concerned with a variety of forms of learning team. Peer tutoring teams operate to help team members to tackle individual projects or tasks, and there is no shared task. Examples of this type of team are described in Section 2.8. Finally, problem-centred teams are used in the context of problem-based courses where a problem rather than a project is the focus of attention. The problem is used as a vehicle for individual learning rather than to produce a team product. Assessment, as in peer tutoring teams and learning teams, is individual. Problem-centred teams are described briefly in Section 2.9. The remainder of Section 2 and of this manual is concerned with project teams.

2.1   Designing tasks for teams

Does the group task require cooperation? How big and complex is the task?

Some group projects involve tasks which can simply be divided up and tackled separately by students who do not need to cooperate with each other. If you believe in the value of group work then the main tasks must require cooperation. Some tasks, although large and complex, are extremely difficult to cooperate on, such as extended essays. Some require both a large group, to cope with the size of the task, and sophisticated teamwork skills, to deal with the organisational complexity, and this will have implications for how much group experience students need and how prominent process variables become.

Are different groups working on the same task?

When different student groups are working on different tasks (for example, sub-components of a very large task, or parallel tasks on related topics) it can be hard to make the tasks of equal size and difficulty so as to ensure reasonable fairness. It can also be hard to ensure that all groups learn similar things. This may not matter if there is no component to the assessment other than the product of group work. But if there is a later exam or if the group work feeds in to later modules, then it makes a great deal of difference what each group task consists of. While it may appear to the lecturer that the whole syllabus has been covered, each group may have dealt with only a small part of it, and this may leave different groups' members in an awkward position. If groups can negotiate the task then this can make it hard for the tutor to calibrate the difficulty of different groups' tasks and to ensure that all groups have tasks which provide opportunities for all members to contribute, learn and gain credit equally. As with all student-centred methods, each additional layer of student centredness and flexibility brings with it additional potential problems.

Does everyone in each group benefit or learn the same?

Even if each group tackles the same task, the individuals within groups may tackle different sub-tasks. What is to stop individual group members from avoiding the very content or skill they should be learning, such as using the computer, analysing the statistics, writing up the report, or avoiding a group skill such as leadership? If one student tackles sub-topic A and another tackles sub-topic B, will either be disadvantaged in their learning or in subsequent assessments involving topics A or B? If group work is superimposed on a tight syllabus or fixed list of learning outcomes it is important to devise group tasks and processes in a way which enables each student to achieve every desired outcome and not just the one they choose to tackle.

2.2   Forming teams

How big should the group be?

The larger the group, the more problems students will have cooperating and coordinating their efforts, the easier it is for students to "hide", and the harder it can be to distinguish the contribution of individuals. Groups larger than six can lead to many problems and few benefits other than a saving in marking time.

How are the groups formed?

If groups are allowed to form themselves there will be groups of friends together. This will improve interaction and cooperation but may mitigate against rigour, self-discipline or being able to tackle difficult group problems. It will also tend to produce groups of good students and a rump of poor students no group wants as members. This may open you up to accusations of unfairness. In work contexts teams seldom select their own membership, and it may be more realistic to allocate students randomly. This will be perceived as more fair and will distribute stronger and weaker students more evenly.

Allocating students on the basis of learning style, preferred group role or other quasi-psychological grounds can be difficult, but it is not impossible. Cuthbert (1994) reports using the popular Belbin "Group roles preference inventory" (see Belbin, 1981) to allocate management students to teams so as to produce groups with a balanced mix of roles, and this produced more successful teams on a variety of courses. Exercise 3 in the *Learning in Teams: A Student Manual* is concerned with such roles and can be used as a basis for this kind of team selection.

You may have good grounds for "rigging"' group membership to cope with individual idiosyncrasies you know about. If there are a succession of assessed group tasks it can be wise to change group membership from time to time so that there is no perception of unfairly carrying the same weaker student or riding on the ability of a strong student repeatedly, or simply having to continue to cope with an unfortunate and incompatible mix.

2.3 Assessing the products of teamwork

It is individuals who gain qualifications, not teams, and some way has to be found to allocate marks fairly to individuals within teams. Simply assigning individuals the same team mark can lead to poor students benefiting from the work of better students (and, vice versa, good students being brought down by poor students). Lazy or strategic students can opt out of their group without penalty. This can lead to justifiable resentment between students. If the group's product is not assessed, however, and individuals are appraised using only conventional methods such as an unseen exam, there is no incentive to take teamwork seriously, and students opt out in order to prepare for the exam. In addition the effect of individuals' efforts being averaged out within groups tends to produce a narrow overall range of marks, and, as group products tend to be better than individual products, higher means. As a consequence, without special additional assessment features the assessment of groups is normally considered thoroughly unsatisfactory.

Limiting the emphasis of the group mark

The problems outlined above may be considered tolerable provided that the group mark does not represent too large a proportion of the total mark for an individual for the course element being assessed – probably no more than 50 per cent of the total marks available. In practice this often involves students contributing an individual report for assessment as well as a written group report or oral group presentation, or sitting an exam in addition to contributing to the group report. Some projects also involve diaries or logs which give the tutor evidence of a student's work throughout the group project, which would not otherwise be open to inspection, and such logs can be assessed or used to moderate individual marks. The additional assessment may have to be designed carefully if it is not to involve excessive marking effort or to lead to students withdrawing their effort from the group work.

Judging students' relative contributions

On some courses tutors feel they have enough information about the way individual students have contributed to their group's work to be able to moderate the group mark to some extent for each individual. For example, if teams work in a lab the tutor may be able to observe students regularly, noting who is present, who is leading and who is doing the work. The most common arrangement is for individual students initially to be allocated the group's mark, and then the tutor moderates this mark up to 10 per cent either way for above or below average contributions, based on observations and notes. However, it is difficult for tutors to gain access to appropriate evidence. Observation of groups in action in class or during supervision sessions is difficult and time-consuming and may provide little valid evidence concerning independent work outside class where most of the work gets done; it is also highly subjective and open to personal bias. Diaries or logs may provide useful additional evidence. Vivas can be used effectively where the size of the project justifies the time involved: it can be possible to judge an individual student's relative contribution to a group report with just a few well chosen questions in a brief viva.

Dividing up the group task

For some projects it may be possible to allocate different sub-elements of the group project to individuals and to apportion at least some of the marks to individuals for the element for which they were personally responsible.

50%		50%		
Individual mark for project component	+	Group mark for entire project	=	Total individual mark

It can sometimes be difficult to divide projects up into elements of equal size, difficulty or ease of marking – for example, background research and creative problem-solving is less visible than oral presentation or report-writing but may be equally important. Also, once students are responsible for separate components they may stop cooperating with one another in order to concentrate on their own piece of work. Fair marks for individuals may be achieved at the expense of good group work and a coherent project report.

These problems disappear if it is possible to use a series of tasks, for each of which members of the team take a different role or undertake a different component of the task. In this way there is rotation round the components, and by the end of the series of tasks every student has taken responsibility for and experienced each component. The organisational chart below illustrates this for projects 1 to 6, each containing six components, involving team members A, B, C, D, E and F.

		Project					
Project Component		1	2	3	4	5	6
1	Literature search and summary	A	B	C	D	E	F
2	Design of study	B	C	D	E	F	A
3	Collection of data	C	D	E	F	A	B
4	Analysis of data	D	E	F	A	B	C
5	Writing of report	E	F	A	B	C	D
6	Oral presentation of report	F	A	B	C	D	E

If it was felt important that students should not work alone or if there were fewer opportunities to run projects, then students could be teamed up within each project, as in this second organisational chart:

Project Component		Project 1	2	3
1	Literature search and summary	A&B	C&D	E&F
2	Design of study	B&C	D&E	F&A
3	Collection of data	C&D	E&F	A&B
4	Analysis of data	D&E	F&A	B&C
5	Writing of report	E&F	A&B	C&D
6	Oral presentation of report	F&A	B&C	D&E

This plan also ensures continuity between each successive stage of each project, in that, in project 1, student B is involved in both stages 1 and 2, student C is involved in both stages 2 and 3, and so on. In this example, A's marks for project 1 could be calculated as follows:

25%		25%		50%		
Mark for project component 1	+	Mark for project component 6	+	Overall project mark	=	Total individual mark

Sharing the group grade

While the tutor may be in the best position to judge the quality of the product of the group work, the group may be in the best position to judge the relative contributions of its members. One way to use their knowledge is to allocate the group product a mark, multiply it by the number of students in the group, and then allow the group to decide for itself how this total should be divided between its members.

Example:
Tutor awards a mark of 60 per cent for a report produced by a team of five students.

The students therefore have 60 x 5 = 300 marks to distribute among themselves.

Any combination which adds up to 300 is acceptable, such as: 50 + 55 + 60 + 65 + 70. Groups who have not thought about the implications of this in advance may contribute very unevenly to the team task but then opt out of the difficult decisions involved in allocating marks and agree to everyone getting the same mark. There can be no accusation of unfairness in this event because the consequences are the students' own responsibility, but this is still not desirable because the assessment method did not successfully encourage even contributions within the team. It is therefore important to consider how this process will operate at the outset and to discuss with students how they will go about dividing up the marks at the end. Students can be asked at the start of their work to list the criteria they will use to divide the marks, and the mechanism they will use to implement these criteria, on a sheet which accompanies a project proposal. It can be helpful, the first time students experience such a process, to provide both criteria and a decision-making mechanism, rather than hoping they will come up with something appropriate and fair on their own. For example:

Team Project Assessment Mechanism

Team project mark x Number of students in team = Total marks available

....   x   ....   = ...

Consider three aspects of individuals' contributions:

1   **Quantity of contributions**
        Attendance at meetings
        Number of tasks taken on
        Size of tasks
        Amount of time spent on tasks
2   **Quality of contributions**
        Completed tasks, on time
        Accurate, error free, little tidying required
        Clear or confusing?
        Imaginative or predictable?
3   **Contribution to team**
        Made suggestions, had good ideas
        Active in meetings, enthusiastic
        Sorted problems, smoothed difficulties
        Helped make decisions and keep to them

Stage 1
        Have a brief open discussion in your team, considering what each
        member in turn contributed. Try to be positive but rigorous.

Stage 2
        On your own, decide for each member of the team, including yourself,
        what mark each should get overall.
        RULES
        1 The total of the marks you give must be the same as the total given
           above.

        2 There must be no more than 20% between the top and the bottom mark.

        3 You are not permitted to give yourself the top mark.

Stage 3
        Average the marks of everyone in the team and write them in the spaces
        below.

        Check that they still add up to the total above.

        All sign to signify your agreement.

Name	Mark	Signature

Total   _____

Peer assessment of contributions

The use of clear criteria and rating scales can provide useful safeguards for the process of differentiating between the contributions of individuals. As above, the tutor allocates a mark for the group product, but the students assess one another's contributions to a list of elements of the project – for example, to background research, data collection, design ideas or whatever. Students may not have the ability to judge how good each team member is in absolute terms, but they are in a good position to tell if they contributed above or below average.

It is possible to weight different elements according to their importance, as in the example below in which collecting and analysing data is considered more important than other aspects of the project. In this example it would be possible for a student who contributed well below average to every aspect of the project to receive a total weighting of −16 per cent. Placing smaller weightings on components would reduce this possible range. The outcome of these peer moderations could also be used as guidance to the tutor, to be taken into account or even acted on in normal circumstances, but need not be binding should the tutor know about victimisation or unfair treatment within a team.

Explaining how everything works to the students at the outset will both make it more likely to work at the end and have a positive impact on group behaviour. A student who knows she will be peer assessed according to her relative contribution to the group's final presentation is unlikely to leave all the presentation to her colleagues. In practice it is rare to find patterns of moderation as extreme as the one in the example, and the impact of moderations is often minimal on final marks but very productive in terms of team behaviour.

Team Project Peer Moderation

Instructions

For each team member in turn, discuss and rate their *relative contribution* to the completion of each component of the team project: did they contribute above or below average within the team? You can't all have contributed above average, so make sure your individual marks average the same as the team mark.

Student name _____

Extent of individual contribution to each component

Component of team project	well below average	below average	average	above average	well above average
1 Literature review	−2	−1	0	<u>+1</u>	+2
2 Design of study	−2	−1	0	+1	<u>+2</u>
3 Collection of data	−4	−2	0	+2	<u>+4</u>
4 Analysis of data	−5	−3	0	<u>+3</u>	+5
5 Writing of report	−2	−1	0	+1	+2
6 Oral presentation of report	−1	0	0	0	+1

Tutor's mark for team project   62%

Sum of moderation marks   +7

Individual mark   69%

Signatures of team members:

Project exams

After a group project is over it is sometimes possible to set an exam question, under conventional examination conditions, to test individual students' knowledge and understanding of the work they undertook during the project. Such questions should be designed so that they can be answered only if the student had been thoroughly involved in the group's work – indeed, any other type of question will encourage students to bail out of their group in order to revise for the exam.

In the example below the students are told in advance about the type of question and that it will be a single compulsory question. The advance briefing is crucial here.

Advance Briefing for Project Exam

In the exam you will be set a single compulsory question based on the site development group project. One major variable or aspect of the situation will be changed and you will be asked to discuss how this would have affected your planning decisions.

You should familiarise yourselves with all aspects of the site and your group's design and planning decisions. You should bring your group report and plans with you to the exam, together with any notes or other documents you will find helpful – but remember you will have little time to consult these so do not bring too much. You will not be allowed to consult with members of your team and will be assessed individually.

Exam Question

In the simulated site development group project you undertook there was an alternative site at the north end of the High Street (marked "B" on your plans). Had this been purchased and developed as a shopping mall by a competing property development company six months before your project began, what effect would this have had on your planning decisions?

Students' performance in this exam can be used in addition to a mark for the group project, to moderate the group mark, or even instead of the group mark where examination regulations require the use of 100 per cent examination assessment.

Hybrids

It is common to mix the above assessment methods in order to limit the possibility of unfairness or bias associated with any one system and to assess a wider range of skills or competencies than any one method alone could achieve. For example, students may obtain 30 per cent of their marks from the section of a final report for which they were personally responsible, 30 per cent from a mark for the whole team report, 15 per cent from a team presentation and 25 per cent from a short individually taken project exam. Some schemes for assessing individuals within teams have become unnecessarily complex and, upon careful scrutiny, have been found to make very little difference to individual students' overall marks compared with a simple team mark. The impact of such carefully developed hybrid schemes may be more on students' perceptions of fairness and on the way they behave within teams than on their marks. The potential for beneficial side-effects of assessment schemes should not be underestimated.

2.4 Assessing the process of teamwork

If teamwork has been introduced in part to develop teamwork skills then these skills, and not just the products of teamwork, should be assessed. It is possible completely to separate the assessment of content and process. Some courses leave all the assessment of the product to the tutor but students then assess the way other individuals have worked in the team. A course at Oxford Brookes University develops students' team skills to the point where key team members are deliberately moved between teams at crucial points (a realistic simulation of the unpredictability of working life) and then are assessed for how well they coped with the disruption.

Identifying skills

Teamwork does not involve a single skill, but many. This is one reason why it is such an effective educational medium. Teamwork can involve:

- selecting team members with complementary skills and styles

- adapting complementary team roles

- behaving cooperatively: as a "team player"

- chairing team meetings

- performing specific team functions (e.g., secretary, ideas person)

- time and task management

- interpersonal influence

- negotiation

- group facilitation

- creative problem-solving (such as brainstorming)

- use of a range of working methods (such as co-consulting).

Each of these skills can be examined and broken up into component elements. For example, chairing meetings involves a whole range of behaviours, illustrated in the checklist for Exercise 22 in *Learning in Teams: A Student Manual*. Checklists such as this can, in effect, form the criteria used in assessing the skills. It is important if you intend to appraise teamwork that you and your students are clear which of the above skills you are assessing.

Direct observation of team behaviour

You can sample the way teams operate, visiting teams for short periods and using checklists to focus your observation. This may be relatively easy during laboratory time or fieldwork but difficult or impossible when students are working in teams during non-timetabled hours in their own chosen workspace.

It can be difficult, though not impossible, for teams to hide weaknesses and "fake good" while you are observing them. However, it is hard not to disrupt teams

16

simply by being there – being observed changes most people's behaviour. There is no guarantee that the skills you wish to observe will be displayed during your visit: for example, they may be quietly getting on with individual tasks, may not be at a creative phase in their work, may not be experiencing interpersonal difficulties which they need to resolve, and so on. It is possible to observe for an hour and see virtually no revealing team behaviour which can be used for assessment. Any one visit may represent a poor sample of the overall way a team works. They may normally work harmoniously and productively and simply be having an off-day when you come to observe them. Also a single visit gives a static impression of a group at one point in their development rather than an overview of dynamic development. As a result you may need to visit several times at several stages to get a fair and revealing impression of their skills, and this can be enormously time-consuming.

Peer review

Teams can be in a good position to review their own behaviour: they are there all the time and experience the consequences of lack of teamwork skills. Groups can assess their own performance using the checklists in *Learning in Teams: A Student Manual*. They should use the checklists individually and then compare their ratings and discuss each point before agreeing on final ratings.

Global assessment

Assessing or giving feedback on individual component skills can be useful as a learning process as it identifies specific behaviours rather than general descriptions, but it involves a reductionist view of teamwork. Does effective teamwork automatically follow from an accumulation of all the behaviours on the checklists, or are there broader-scale issues which are more important? It may also be too detailed and time-consuming to use to derive marks from. There probably shouldn't be a mechanical procedure for translating numerical ratings into grades, but a global grade based on criteria of the following kind.

Grade	Criterion
A	Team has made appropriate and effective use of a wide range of team skills and processes.
	All team members have completed agreed tasks to a high standard and on time.
	Team has identified and overcome teamwork problems effectively and with insight.
	Team has developed as a team, experimenting with and mastering a range of new team processes.
B	Team has made use of a number of team skills and processes, most of which were reasonably effective.
	Most team members have completed agreed tasks, to a good standard and on time.
	Some team problems diagnosed and addressed; a few problems remain.
	Team has developed the team and tried a few new processes.
C	Some team skills and processes tried, some of which were effective.
	Most members have completed most tasks, though not always well or on time.
	Some team problems identified and tackled, though not always effectively.
	Some development as a team but plenty of scope for further improvement.
D	Team has encountered difficulties (such as individuals not attendin, or contributing, unresolved disagreements, getting well behind schedule) which it has tended to avoid or has not yet overcome.
	Major components of agreed teamwork are incomplete.
	Little development of team or of team skills despite a few efforts to improve.
F	Team no longer intact as a team.
	Team task not completed.

Individual assessment

Individuals may contribute unevenly and possess very different levels of teamwork skills but still receive the same team grade. The following kind of peer assessment form can be employed to identify the extent to which each individual in a team possesses team skills and contributes to the effective functioning of the team. This can be used to moderate individual marks around the team mark for the product of the team project.

Peer Assessment of Team Skills

Instructions

For each team member in turn, discuss and rate their *relative contribution* to the effective functioning of the team: did they contribute above or below average within the team? You can't all have contributed above average, so make sure your individual marks average the same as the team mark.

Student name --

Extent of individual contribution to each component

Aspect of team functioning	well below average	below average	average	above average	well above average
1 Forming good team cohesion	−2	−1	0	<u>+1</u>	+2
2 Leadership, managing meetings	<u>−2</u>	−1	0	+1	+2
3 Planning and allocating tasks	−2	<u>−1</u>	0	+1	+2
4 Generating ideas and solutions	−2	−1	<u>0</u>	+1	+2
5 Tackling team social problems	−2	−1	0	+1	<u>+2</u>
6 Organising individuals to do jobs	−2	<u>−1</u>	0	+1	+2
7 Helping team members to finish jobs	−2	<u>−1</u>	0	+1	+2
8 Willingly taking on unpopular jobs	−2	−1	<u>0</u>	+1	+2

Tutor's mark for team project report   58%

Sum of moderation marks   −2

Individual mark   56%

Signatures of team members:

Setting up and assessing teamwork

Teamwork logs: assessing reflection on and awareness of team skills

What may be more important to the development of teamwork skills is not so much observable behaviour as students' ability to recognise team problems when they see them, diagnose them, act to do something about them, and check whether the new way of operating is working. It may be this active effort to try to improve which has more impact than the use of any specific technique or behaviour. This is a more dynamic and forward-looking view of teamwork.

Though this kind of behaviour is very hard to observe, it is possible for students to document. Students can be asked to keep a "Teamwork Log" in which they regularly write reflective notes on the way the team is operating. This log can then be used as the main resource for a final report.

A teamwork report can involve students answering the following questions.

1. What steps have you taken to organise your teamwork?

2. What steps have you taken to monitor the effectiveness of your team?

3. What steps have you taken to improve the effectiveness of your team?

4. What problems have you encountered in working as a team and how did you tackle them?

5. If you were able to embark on a second, similar task as a team, what would be different about the way you go about working, and why?

These questions could be used as the basis of criteria and marks as in the form overleaf.

Assessment of Teamwork Reports

Grades: A =   Outstanding

              B =   Very good

              C =   Good

              D =   Limited but adequate

              F =   Limited but inadequate, or missing

	Criterion	Grade				
1	The range and appropriateness of organisational steps and strategies adopted	A	B	C	D	F
2	The range and usefulness of methods used to monitor effectiveness, and the quality of evidence obtained	A	B	C	D	F
3	The range and effectiveness of steps taken to improve team performance	A	B	C	D	F
4	The perceptiveness with which team problems were identified/diagnosed	A	B	C	D	F
5	The range, appropriateness and effectiveness of steps taken to overcome problems	A	B	C	D	F
6	The quality of review and action planning for a second team task.	A	B	C	D	F

You may well need to train students to be more aware of what goes on in teams, and *Learning in Teams: A Student Manual* is designed to do exactly that.

For formal assessment purposes you can:

- ask teams to submit a team process report on completion of their work

- require such a report as one section of a team project report

- require individuals to submit their own individual team process reports

- hold short vivas with either whole teams or each member of a team, asking questions about their operation as a team

- use an exam question of the form: "Give an account of the way your team strove to operate effectively. What general issues emerged about the operation of teams? What steps might you personally take to address these issues next time you work in a team?" You can even warn students in advance that they will get such an exam question – the only way they can "revise" for it is to reflect on the operation of their team and find out more about explanations and alternatives!

2.5 Reporting the outcomes of teamwork

The most common forms of outcome of teamwork are written reports, presentations, posters and exhibitions, vivas, exams, and portfolios or log books. Each have their advantages and disadvantages.

Written reports

Written reports are the most common mode of outcome. Their form is usually familiar to both students and tutors, and the reliability of marking, although poor, is usually considered acceptable. It is possible to arrange for individuals to have distinct responsibility for components of written reports and external examiners can read them at their leisure. As teams can undertake larger and more complex projects than individuals, team reports can easily grow to colossal proportions unless strict size limits are applied. As much teamwork simulates work practices and reports outside higher education are usually much briefer than academic reports this should not pose too much of a problem, though students may find reducing all their individual work to a succinct team report challenging.

Presentations

Team presentations are common, and they can succeed in developing presentation skills and provide a public forum which usually motivates students and affords a very real deadline for completion. Coherent team presentations with every team member actively involved are unusual – it is more common to see the team member with the best presentation skills dominate or for the whole to be less than the sum of the parts. Reliable assessment is difficult, and without careful use of ratings against specified criteria it is easy for marks to be excessively influenced by slickness of presentation rather than conceptual sophistication, especially if peer assessment is involved. External examiners cannot see much of this outcome without time-consuming use of video to provide indications of overall standards. It is very

22

difficult to allocate marks differentially to individuals after a team presentation. If the project has been very substantial the team will have a great deal to report, and this leads to either tediously long or rushed and superficial presentations. If there are many teams the sequence of presentations can drag on a bit and an audience can be difficult to rustle up without using assessment penalties for leverage. Overall, presentations may be best used as interesting add-ons for making outcomes public and building in demands for additional skills rather than as providing a suitable basis for substantial contributions to marks. Some projects use them to moderate marks for written reports rather than as sources of marks in their own right.

Posters and exhibitions

Posters can provide a quick and illuminating vehicle for communicating the outcome of project work and are particularly good for quick sharing between teams. Students are usually unfamiliar with the use of posters or have poor poster presentation skills, so anyone with proficient graphic skills can obtain good marks relatively easily because the overall standard is low. It is difficult for eight students genuinely to cooperate on the production of a single A1-sized poster, and this is usually obvious in the end-product. Exactly what a "degree standard" poster should look like is unclear, whereas the appropriate standard for written work is relatively well understood and widely shared. Posters may therefore be best used for the reporting of short projects allocated relatively few marks, or as adjuncts to other more reliable methods, rather than as the only assessment device for a course.

Exhibitions are widely used for assessing individual work in creative areas such as architecture, and standards and presentation skills are better developed there. Exhibitions can also be suitable for design work in engineering and other forms of project work with visual elements. However, there are still problems associated with distinguishing the contribution of individuals to joint exhibitions. At the minimum there should be an associated viva (or "crit") associated with the exhibition to explore issues it raises and to distinguish between individuals.

Vivas

Vivas can be very useful to get behind the surface of neatly presented reports to the reality of team members' understanding and involvement. Either individual or team vivas need not be very long to provide valuable information, as they can be applied flexibly to probe areas of uncertainty. However, to provide the basis of reliable marks they need to be reasonably long and undertaken to a standard format. They are therefore best used to moderate individual marks from a team average or to moderate a team mark from that derived from a written report. External examiners cannot easily see the contents of a viva and are unlikely to want to be directly involved. Vivas are unlikely to be suitable in any circumstances without the back up of a report or other written evidence. Because they involve a fair investment in time they are best reserved for very substantial projects where the assessment weighting justifies the additional attention to reliability and individual marks.

Exams

Project exams can be a very effective way of distinguishing between individual students within teams provided that they ask the type of question which can only be answered on the basis of involvement in the team task and do not encourage bailing out of the team in order to revise. They can use relatively short questions which are much quicker to mark than extended reports. Students should be allowed to take their project report into their exam with them to avoid the absurdity of having to memorise its contents and in order to allow more advanced questions. If set as the only form of assessment project exams wreck team-work, and they should be used only in conjunction with assessment of a team report or other team product.

Portfolios or log books

Portfolios are collections of intermediate products as a project progresses, such as sketches, draft plans and outlines, and logs are detailed records of work undertaken, often including reflection and informal notes. They both offer great potential as assessment devices because they bring learning and assessment so close together and can be so revealing about the quality of teamwork. They can also be used to distinguish individuals within teams if each member keeps a log. Team logs are difficult to produce, though team portfolios containing draft designs and so on can be useful. The problems lie with reliability of assessment and the difficulty of defining what kind of material should be included. As soon as a log is assessed it becomes an invitation to "fake good" rather than a genuine vehicle for reflection, and there are inevitable confusions of function and disagreements about whether students should include, for example, failed designs or incorrect analyses. It takes very careful specification of assessment criteria and serious attention to developing students' ability to use logs appropriately before they can be relied on as the sole source of marks. They are often best used as additional sources of information to moderate team marks based on a more conventional product such as a report or to moderate individual marks above or below team marks based on a report.

2.6   Other design issues

What are the aims of the group work?

Is the quality of the product of group work most important, or does the process matter as well? And if the process is important, is it project work skills or group work skills which are most important? Assessment of group project work often runs into difficulties because it concentrates on aspects which were not of central importance to either the tutor or the students. The aims should be made explicit, and prioritised, before the assessment methods are designed and criteria agreed.

What fail-safe mechanisms are there?

Groups may collapse due to intractable personality clashes or illness of key members. Projects, especially those devised by students themselves, may turn out to be unmanageable in the time. Individuals may, for whatever reason, entirely fail to come up with the goods for their key part of an interlocking whole. Should everyone in the group suffer lower marks or even fail because of this? You may need ground rules to fall back on, just as there are rules in the eventuality of individual illness during final exams. With group work, however, the implications may be more far-reaching. Most lecturers experience fewer disasters than they originally anticipate, but it is reassuring for students to know what the fail-safe position is and this may reduce resistance. Some tutors allow themselves to intervene quite subjectively if they feel that an individual or group has been unfairly disadvantaged, and students may find this encouraging or alarming depending on their trust in the tutor.

Do students understand the assessment from the start?

The way the assessment of groups works affects student behaviour right from the start – in choice of groups, in the degree of cooperation, competition and responsibility, and so on. Having a well worked out system for dividing marks fairly will not have the desired effect if it is not introduced until after groups have submitted their work. It is vital that students understand right from the outset exactly how marks will be allocated. This might involve their being involved in applying or even negotiating criteria, or hearing accounts from past students of how it works.

Where do students get the skills from to work in groups?

Students who have never worked in groups before can struggle badly and fail to produce anything worth while. I am not talking here about awareness of group dynamics or sophisticated group facilitation skills but the practical basics of getting a group task completed to a deadline: appointing a note-taker to record decisions or setting a time for the next meeting. Students need to learn to undertake small tasks in small groups before tackling extended tasks in groups bigger than four, and they require practical advice and opportunities to reflect on group experiences.

Students deserve a trial run at unassessed group work before being appraised in a way which contributes towards their degree, and may need trial runs at any peer assessment process involved as well. Even if the development of group skills is not a priority a modest investment in developing such skills will improve student performance and make assessment of the products of group work fairer and more valid.

How is an appropriate distribution of marks achieved?

Groups tend to produce better work than individuals, and so group work tends to produce higher average marks than individual work. Also the effect of putting mixed students together in groups is to make groups less varied than individuals – producing a narrower spread of marks between groups than between individuals. The common outcome is a high mean and a low standard deviation with no fails. If this is unacceptable then steps need to be taken to manipulate grading in some way.

Markers can adjust their standards subjectively over time (just as coursework marking needs to use different standards from exam marking to avoid much higher marks in the former than the latter). Rating scales linked to criteria can be used which shift the mid-point in the scale downwards to change the relationship between judgements and marks. Any of the methods described above to allocate marks to individuals will have the effect of increasing variation between students, and some (such as the use of project exams) will also reduce averages.

Are there intermediate deadlines?

As with extended project work, extended group work can benefit from intermediate deadlines and intermediate assessment – of plans, progress reports or drafts of final reports – as a way of guiding progress and keeping groups on track. An opportunity to review the operation of the group and compare it with others is also valuable before things go too wrong or in time to make productive changes to working practices.

Are students involved in assessment?

It is very common when group work is evaluated to involve students in peer assessment of other groups' work or within groups of other students' contributions.

This is not necessary, however, and should not be introduced without a specific purpose. It is sensible to separate assessment of the quality of products (which the tutor may be in the best position to judge) from assessment of process (which students may be in the best position to judge).

2.7   Learning teams

There are considerable advantages in turning any group that meets regularly for discussion into a supportive learning team. If the students in the group know one another they are more likely to feel comfortable about contributing to class discussions, to discuss work outside class hours and to share scarce resources. Within courses where students spend little time in the institution, especially when what little time they do spend is in the classroom, establishing learning support teams can be particularly valuable. All that may be required is to give the students a chance to get to know one another, a way of getting in touch with one another, some ideas about how they can help one another and the reassurance that this is a recognised and valuable thing to do.

Tutorial groups as learning teams

The most obvious framework for establishing supportive learning teams is within tutorial or seminar groups. When a tutorial or seminar group meets for the first time it can be helpful to include the following components.

- Introduce group members to one another and to you. You might ask students to interview each other in pairs for five minutes to obtain a biography, including what each individual is hoping to get out of the course. Then ask the members of each pair to report the other person's biography to the whole group. Students can wear name labels for the first one or two meetings until they get to know one another.

- Discuss with the students "ground rules" for the seminar or tutorial sessions and make sure these are known and accepted by everyone. For example:

  – prereading must be completed by all students attending the tutorial and there will be a quick check what everyone has read at the beginning of each meeting

  – seminar presentations must be supported by overheads or hand outs and not just read out from a paper

  – everyone will be punctual and not arrive late or leave early in a way which will disrupt the learning of the group

  – sexist and racist language and attitudes will not be tolerated; criticism should be constructive.

- Pass a list around the group and invite all students to add their names and phone numbers. Have the list copied and distribute it to the participating members.

- Encourage the group to arrange at least one social meeting outside normal hours and outside the university.

At the group's second meeting use a team-building exercise. Reinforce team-building for ten minutes at each group meeting. A short activity can be undertaken

26

which is designed to get different clusters of students talking to one another about course content. Ground rules for the group can be reviewed from time to time and the list of tutorial group members updated. An account of a one-day induction event for setting up such learning teams for an Italian course can be found in Gibbs (1992b).

Learning teams within large groups

Where there are no or infrequent tutorial groups, where the smallest size of class meeting is too large for close social grouping (i.e., 16 and above) or where students on a modular course have no stable peer group because everyone is taking a different combination of options, it may be more appropriate to create special learning teams which do not meet in class time at all. This may be especially useful for part-time students, who may come into the university only once a week for lectures. A training day held during the induction period can be used very effectively to build learning teams. Students may be organised by the lecturer taking the course into teams on the basis of geography, similar employment or whatever shared characteristics seem appropriate. Once again the students need to be introduced to one another, get to know one another, do team-building exercises, agree on ground rules for the groups and settle on a mechanism for keeping in touch. Once the framework exists the students will work together, change groups or, in a few cases, decide not to participate, but if no framework is offered only the most confident students will create one for themselves. Within a large group teams of from five to eight work best. If the teams are any larger, organisation is too unwieldy. If they are any smaller, there is the risk that drop-outs will destroy the group.

On a part-time business studies degree programme of 90 first-year students at the University of Central England, learning teams (or "study networks", as they called them) were established as the first activity on a course which otherwise provided little opportunity for student interaction. They helped students' motivation and commitment to their learning and the course and developed and enriched academic performance. Students shared books, read one another's essays, helped with copies of lecture notes when one of the team was ill, and so on. They met largely outside the university and outside of normal hours. One year after they were set up, 92 per cent of the students involved were still members of a study group and 94 per cent thought that study networks should be encouraged on the course (Hartley and Bahra, 1992).

Learning teams for mature students

Mature students often feel isolated and lack confidence at the beginning of a university course. They may need to rush home or to work as soon as lectures are over and may feel awkward among groups who all have recent school experience and a common youth culture; they doubt the value of their life and work experience in a new and intimidating environment. They can benefit greatly from learning teams set up specifically for them in a particular course or discipline. These can be established in much the same way as described above except that, where the students would not normally spend any time together as a group, they need a mechanism for getting together and getting to know one another so that team-building, organisation for maintaining contact and guide-lines for ways of helping one another can be developed. This can be initiated by arranging a meeting of interested students at a time when there are no lectures, or as a follow-up to

27

induction workshops. Most mature students are very keen to be involved in anything that is likely to offer academic and social support at the beginning of the year, and if groups can be established early, with provision for including those who would have difficulty making contacts on their own, they are likely to survive the pressure of work, which increases as the year goes on.

A member of academic staff, student services staff or student organisations can advertise and convene a preliminary meeting within the first two weeks of the start of the academic year. At this meeting students can be introduced to one another and the idea of learning teams can be discussed. Names and addresses of those interested in joining in can be taken down and a follow-up training session arranged for the same time the next week. Students can also be given handouts on working in teams and team-building exercises.

At their second meeting the students can choose their own groups on the basis of shared interests, geography, timetable or concerns about their work, do team-building exercises, record the names, addresses and phone numbers of other members of their team and arrange a regular meeting place. The person organising the teams may be able to help find this on campus or, if the groups are arranged geographically, the students may arrange a place of their own.

The organiser should keep a record of group membership, and which groups are meeting where, so that other students can be added to the groups if they wish and the organiser can act as a link in emergencies and trouble-shoot if necessary.

2.8 Peer tutoring teams

Peer tutoring teams fall half way between learning teams and project teams. Usually the students are involved in individual project work or work experience, but peer tutoring teams are set up to support their individual work. This involves a different kind of cooperation than in team project work where a task is shared. The following examples, drawn from Bochner et al. (1995), illustrate a range of applications of peer tutoring teams.

At Falmouth College of Art and Design, graphic information design students who undertake individual project work and who are traditionally supervised individually, are formed into teams. These teams are trained to use criteria to critique one another's work and provide a supportive context for reporting on progress, getting reactions to early design ideas, and so on. This encourages less isolated work and, on account of the establishment of close relationships within the teams, a less threatening end-point when students' design work is reviewed at the final public "crit".

A large and fast growing BA in business studies at Anglia Polytechnic University employs two peer support mechanisms to cope with the burden of dissertation supervision. First, third-year students who have just finished their dissertations are used to brief second-year students who are about to start planning theirs. Second, students tackling related topics are put together in dissertation support teams so that they can discuss their work with others who will understand and be interested in what they are doing.

At Auckland University postgraduate students undertaking Masters degrees by research are supported in forming self-help teams in which they discuss their progress and problems. Many of these groups mix students from different subject areas where all they have in common is that they are undertaking extended independent research, but this is still invaluable.

On a business and finance HND course at Anglia Polytechnic University, instead of work placement tutors spending a great deal of time with each individual student, the students are recalled periodically to special one-day team sessions where they share their work experiences. Sharing and reflecting on work experiences and problems with peers enables the members of a large group to gain some familiarity with a variety of situations and experiences in the field, so expanding their repertoire and awareness. Students act as consultants to one another in these team meetings.

2.9 Problem-centred teams

Problem-based learning usually involves students working cooperatively in teams, though they are problem-centred rather than task-centred and are not usually assessed as a team. Problem-based learning in medicine at McMaster University, for example, involves students meeting in problem classes of eight students with a tutor for three hours a week, and the eight cooperate in their learning between these tutored meetings. Students undertake all their studying in such problem-centred teams. All formal assessment is, however, individual. As a more modest example, at a Midlands university, mathematics students meet in autonomous mathematics problem teams once a week. The structure to the meetings is provided by the requirement to submit "minutes" of the sessions, which are handled like committee meetings. The students appoint a chair and a secretary who takes the minutes; these roles rotate at each meeting. An agenda is drawn up consisting of the problems and topics the members of the team want to work on at the meeting, and they then run through the agenda helping one another out. These are not learning teams, in that they do not meet or interact for support purposes outside of these formal sessions. And they are not project teams, because their assignments are still undertaken individually and they do not cooperate on major tasks together. But they do provide support for each other in these weekly seminar team meetings.

Problem-based learning often involves special processes unique to the type of course design and problem involved, and this specialist type of learning will not be considered further here.

Setting up and assessing teamwork

Powerful ideas to guide the development of learning in teams

3.1   Training, demand, monitoring and assessment

Implementing effective development of teamwork skills involves the following four elements.

Training

If students lack a skill then they cannot suddenly use it, and they often start from such a low base-line that they need help before they can even start. If you are asking students to use a new skill, such working in a team, for the first time, it makes sense to start with some training. As training processes involve experience, it can sometimes be interesting to start with an experience "from cold": for example, trying to tackle a short team task without help. This will highlight the extent of students' learning needs and may reveal some skills transferred from other situations. However, it can also be very discouraging. Students' first attempts at teamwork, just like their their first seminar presentations, can be depressingly bad. Students should not be left to struggle for long before being trained.

Demand

Students need to practise skills and courses need to make demands that give them that practice. They should be asked to work in teams whenever possible: to undertake lab work, to share seminar presentations, to tackle fieldwork together, and so on. The issue of demand is related to the issue of "time on task". Students need to have learning time allocated to the development of the skill. If you simply tell them that they should spend time on developing their teamwork skills it obviously isn't going to happen. The easiest way to get students to do this is to allocate class time, to set assignments and to devise learning activities which involve the use of the skills.

Monitoring

Skills seldom develop suddenly or in one go. Most development does not take place in skill training exercises but afterwards, and continues gradually over a long period. Students progressively "tune up" their skills. They do this primarily through noticing what works and what doesn't, experimenting and getting feedback on the consequences. Students who lack skill also tend to lack any way of noticing what works or judging effectiveness. They need ways of monitoring and to get into the habit of reviewing their effectiveness. Among the most useful materials in *Learning in Teams: A Student Manual* are those involving checklists which students can use to monitor and self-assess aspects of their own team behaviour and performance. In teamwork social conventions tend to obstruct open review of performance, and such checklists can be particularly helpful.

30

Assessment

Students can be very strategic, noticing what counts and what is rewarded. Given the excessive size of most curricula, reading lists and so on, they need to be "selectively negligent", choosing what to leave out and what to focus on. This is in itself a valuable transferable skill, and students who lack this awareness of cues as to what counts in courses fare very badly. Most conventional assessment processes do not indicate that skills matter. If you want students to take teamwork skills seriously then you need to identify and assess them.

Also, if we are serious about the role of skills in our curricula, then students' grades and degree classifications should indicate something about how skilful they are, and not just something about what they know. In teamwork it is tempting to pretend that assessing the product of teamwork also assesses the process – but this isn't really so. Teamwork skills need to be judged separately.

If any one of the elements is missing then there can be severe consequences. I have seen a course in which the demands on students to use new skills were considerable: in their first term they had to work in teams of eight to study a small business. Through this they were supposed to develop teamwork skills, but all that they discovered was that teams can be hell. Without any initial training in teamwork the students lacked a way of making progress.

I have seen teamwork projects which contained excellent training exercises but which were followed by content-oriented courses that made almost no demand on students to display the teamwork skills they had developed, and which then fell into disuse.

Courses sometimes go to the trouble of providing some initial skills training and then make demands on students to use these skills, but provide no follow-up support. Although the demand is there, students are not encouraged to pay attention to developing the application of the skill. The need just to get the group task done takes over, and individuals forget about needing to be reflective about their use of skills. Practice alone does not make perfect.

A lack of appropriate assessment can undermine otherwise well thought-out initiatives. For example, students can be trained in teamwork skills, can be required to work in teams, and can take part in regular workshops designed to help them to improve the effective operation of their teams. However, if the assessment consists of an individual report or a conventional exam, then students have no incentive to take teamwork seriously and will concentrate on private, competitive study. If skills are not assessed then students soon stop taking the skill, and skills development exercises and courses, seriously.

Sometimes teamwork is repeatedly assessed without there being any noticeable improvement in team skills. This can happen when feedback comments are either very limited or solely concerned with product of the teamwork. Ideally assessment should provide students with feedback about their team skills, and there should be mechanisms which encourage them to reflect on this feedback and modify their future practices. This might involve student self-assessment.

3.2   The experiential learning cycle

Students do not become proficient in the use of a skill such as how to learn in teams simply by being told about it, discussing it or thinking about it – they have to practise the skill. But practice, on its own, is also ineffective. It is necessary to notice what went well or not so well and to reflect on this and why it happened. It is necessary to develop an "informal theory" or personal explanation of what is going on and what being skilful consists of. And this informal theory needs to be used to help to make decisions next time about what to do differently.

Learning skills involves a four-stage cycle:

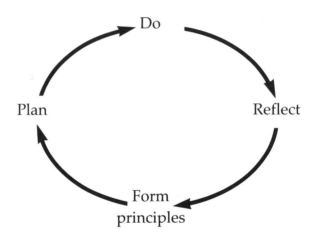

This is the "experiential learning cycle" – a model of how theory is related to practice in learning by doing. You can start anywhere you like on the cycle – with a new experience, with reflections on past experiences, with theory, or with planning to tackle a new situation – as long as you progress round the cycle in the right direction. Teaching and learning processes associated with each stage of the cycle include:

Doing	experiential exercises, actually using teamwork skills
Reflecting	watching a video of your team in action, discussing what happened, using a checklist to assess the use of a various teamwork skills, keeping a reflective log or diary
Forming principles	listening to a lecture about a skill, reading, summarising general principles from a discussion
Planning	preparing for a presentation or for teamwork, setting action plans, identifying priorities for skill development using a profile.

3.3   Team skills development checklist

The following checklist may help to diagnose where you might focus your attention in developing your students' teamwork skills.

Tick

☐   Do students feel the need to become better at working in teams?

☐   Are students given advice about working in teams?

☐   Are students given examples of how effective teams work?

☐   Are students given initial training in teamwork?

☐   Are students given a chance to practise working in teams?

☐   Is the practice "safe" for students so that they can experiment (e.g., not assessed)?

☐   Are students encouraged to experiment with new ways of working?

☐   Is attention paid to the emotional climate within which learning to work in teams operates?

☐   Do students get feedback on their team skills?

☐   Do students get the chance to work in different kinds of team on different kinds of task?

☐
☐   Are students encouraged to follow a "recipe" in working in teams, or to become flexible?

3.4   How teams grow

Teams seem to develop in a particular way, following a predictable pattern. If you can recognise the features of this development in your own team this can help you to understand what is going on and to do something appropriate to help your team to move on to the next stage in its growth.

The life of teams can be described in four stages.

Forming: getting together and getting to know each other, characterised by tentativeness, politeness and anxiety on the part of individuals. At this stage you are not yet really a team and you will hardly have thought about the task you need to get on with.

Storming: this involves arguments about how you are going to operate, who is in charge, who is going to do what, and so on. This is where genuine differences of values and opinions come to the surface and get thrashed out and where personalities clash – sometimes acrimoniously.

Norming: this is where you start to work out the way you are going to cooperate together, and what your ground rules are and where agreements are made.

Performing: this is where, at last, you get on with the task and start getting some productive work done.

Teams often cannot get to the performing stage without going through storming and norming. Without getting important differences out in the open students may never build agreements on solid ground, and teams which have tried to bypass these stages may break up or experience storming at a late and damaging stage. The needs of individuals, the team and the task are emphasised differently at each stage, as illustrated in the diagram below. As you can see, task needs do not become dominant until individual and team needs have been paid attention to. You may never be fully effective in tackling tasks until these individual and team needs have been met.

Relative influence of individual, team and task needs on team members' behaviour at different stages of team development			
Stage of team development	Individual needs	Team needs	Task needs
Forming	High	Medium	Low
Storming	High	High	Low
Norming	Medium	High	Medium
Performing	Medium	Medium	High

Pedler (1986) describes five stages through which groups go in terms of the phases of the task on which they are engaged:

- making contact

- exploration

- getting down to it

- work

- finishing.

Groups can disband or fall apart at the transitions between any of these stages. The end of each stage represents a crisis, and groups may need targeted tutorial support at these times to help them to move on smoothly.

3.5 Progressive development of team skills

Students do not learn teamwork skills all in one go the first time they encounter a team task. It takes considerable experience with a variety of types of task in a variety of teams before students have even had the opportunity to develop good skills. Even then experience on its own will not develop sound skills unless these are explicitly paid attention to, assessed and rewarded. As a consequence it is not realistic for an individual lecturer within an individual module to attempt to develop teamwork. It takes a coordinated approach involving progressive development over a period of time and, inevitably, over a sequence of courses.

This may involve a plan such as that outlined overleaf, for a geology degree.

Year 1

Semester 1

First profiling meeting with personal tutor includes review of team experience and skills.

Core module involves a short team task for teams of three: no assessment of product or team skills.

In parallel all students take a module entitled "Studying Geology" which includes among a range of technical and transferable skills a team skill development exercise and the establishment of a learning team to support all first-year studies.

Semester 2

Core module involves a modest lab-based project for teams of four where the product counts 25% of module marks. A reflective report on teamwork is not assessed but is discussed in a project debriefing seminar. Focus is on reviewing team skills.

Second profiling meeting with personal tutor includes review of team experience and skills.

Year 2

Semester 3

Core module involves a team fieldwork project over several weeks. Individual reports are written up for 75% of the marks with a team report about the team skills involved which counts 25% of the module marks. Focus on managing complex tasks in teams.

Semester 4

Several optional modules use team projects of various kinds requiring library research, each involving marks for the team product and peer assessment of contributions to the team, using a standard procedure and set of criteria. Focus on team research and team writing.

Third profiling meeting with personal tutor includes review of team experience and skills.

Year 3

Semester 5

Major fieldwork project undertaken in large teams with individual components assessed and the overall team map appraised as a team product. Several team skill development exercises while working in the field. Focus on taking on team roles.

Semester 6

Several modules involve various team tasks, all of which include an individual reflective essay on team skills allocated 25% of the marks. Integrated focus on all aspects of teamwork.

Fourth and final profiling meeting with personal tutor includes summary of team experience and skills for completed profile.

Teamwork development exercises

This section contains a summary of the 27 exercises from *Learning in Teams: A Student Manual.* This manual is designed so that student teams can use it to develop their effectiveness and to learn about teams without taking up tutor or classroom time. However, some briefing and encouragement from the tutor can help, and an occasional classroom exercise can demonstrate how to use the manual and show how much can be gained from undertaking the exercises it contains. Students find it particularly useful to compare their own team with others and to talk about how their own team operates in confidence with individuals from other teams. If you run classroom sessions based on these exercises the following tips may be useful.

- Tutors don't have to be experts in teamwork to help students to develop their teamwork skills. The *Student Manual* contains all the expertise students are likely to need and the exercises largely run themselves.

- Each team needs their own copy of the manual out of class as well as in class. It is common for each individual to be lent or sold a copy of the brief *Student Guide* and for each team to be lent or sold a copy of the manual. It is not necessary for every individual to have a copy of the manual.

- It is relatively easy to run even quite large workshops with such well structured materials, with students working as a rule in sub-groups in their teams. Even 60 students in ten teams of six should be perfectly feasible with the teams working in parallel and the tutors' role being to brief each stage of the exercise, watch the time and draw some common issues out at the end.

- Where possible there should be concrete outcomes in terms of action plans. Whatever the exercise the session can finish off with each team in turn reporting, using sentence stem prompts such as:

  "One thing we have realised about the way we work is ..."

  "One thing we are going to do differently in order to be more effective is ..."

  "One exercise from the manual we will work on together (or one further step we will take to examine and improve our team functioning) is ..."

- In general more will be extracted from the exercises if individuals within teams work on the checklists and other tasks they contain separately before the team as a whole comes together for discussion, as this will raise differences and alternative perspectives which unstructured team discussion often hides.

- In general more will be extracted by each team working through exercises separately before teams exchange outcomes with one another, as this will generate a wider range of perceptions and plans than unstructured discussion between teams.

• It can sometimes be useful for students to work in "cross-over groups" rather than in their own team when analysing their team's behaviour and effectiveness, as this gives more freedom, through confidentiality, to say what is actually going on, and also some emotional distance to be more objective. Cross-over groups are made up of one member of each team, as illustrated in the diagram below.

```
    1  1        2  2      3           2  1   3   2  1   3   2  1   3
  1      1    2      2   3    3  3
    1  1        2  2       3    3    3   4  6 5   4  6 5   4  6 5
                           3

    4  4       5  5         6         2  1   3   2  1   3   2  1   3
  4             5    5    6    6  6
    4  4  4    5    5  5    6    6    4  6 5   4  6 5   4  6 5
                   5          6
```

After students have worked in cross-over groups they return to their own team and should be given time to have a "round" involving each person briefly reporting back on something useful from the discussion in their cross-over group. It can be very effective to explain what cross-over groups are early on in the life of a team project and to set up "permanent" cross-over groups solely for the purpose of reviewing team functioning. Every so often in a class session you can announce:

"OK, please quickly get into your cross-over groups and briefly review how your teams are functioning and compare your progress and ways of working with other teams. You have just 15 minutes. Then when you go back into your own teams everyone should make one suggestion about how the team should continue, based on what they have picked up from other teams."

• Only a limited amount can be achieved in classroom exercises. Most development will take place out of class as teams experiment with different ways of working and allocating team roles, tasks, and so on, and notice what works and what doesn't. The main goal of classroom exercises should be, first, to establish a pattern of monitoring and reflection which the teams will continue for themselves. This involves "modelling" what such monitoring and reflection consists of (and here the exercises and checklists in the manual provide ideal support). Second, classroom exercises should intrigue students in the process as opposed to the content of their team project and help them to recognise how important it is to the success of their project. If they find the process of teamwork engaging then they will continue to focus on this without your support.

• Many of the exercises are short and are best undertaken quickly and frequently (for example, reviewing meetings for two minutes each time they finish) rather than ponderously only once.

The remainder of this section summarises the exercises you may wish to use and recommend. As you are unlikely to use all 27 exercises, the following advice is offered on selecting key exercises at key stages.

- It is particularly important for teams to be set up properly. If they don't get off on the right foot it can be vary hard for them to recover. Put a little time aside for Exercise 4 or 7.

- Being organised is absolutely vital, and disorganised teams rarely fulfil their potential. Try Exercise 11 or 13 to help students to decide who should be doing what and when.

- Team meetings which get work done are not like chats, and students will need to learn how to run efficient meetings. Try asking teams to follow the guidelines in Exercise 14 and use Exercise 15 to check that their meetings are working OK.

- Most teams suffer from friction and inappropriate behaviour from some or all of their members, and it can be difficult to raise and tackle issues about people's behaviour. Exercise 20 will help them to identify and bring out into the open what is going wrong, and Exercise 23 will help them to tackle problems once they have identified them.

- Reporting the outcome of teamwork is not the same as students writing on their own. Exercise 25 will help them to write together and Exercise 24 provides advice on team presentations.

4.1   What it's all for

Exercise 1:   *Defining the team task*

This exercise concentrates on the demands of the project – the intended product, criteria for assessment, deadlines, components of the project task, and so on. It involves a checklist for the team to go though. This checklist can provide a useful reminder to you, the tutor, when setting up the project and the tasks and assessment involved.

Exercise 2:   *What we want out of this team*

Not all teams want to get the best possible marks: some want it to be enjoyable or for there to be scope for individuals to explore what they are interested in whether or not it is strictly to do with the project. This exercise helps teams to clarify what they want out of the project and the team. If this is not sorted out early on it can trip students up later.

4.2   Forming a team

As discussed in Section 2.3 above, the formation of teams may be out of students' control. But if they have any say in the matter this exercise will help them to make appropriate decisions.

Exercise 3:   *Who to work with*

Friendship or even general ability can be a poor basis for team selection. This exercise uses Belbin's (1981) characterisation of team roles to help individuals recognise their strengths and weaknesses as team members and so to form teams with balanced strengths. Without such considerations teams can end up full of "innovators" with no "finishers", or all "team workers" and no "leaders", "shapers" or "organisers" – disastrous mixtures!

4.3   Developing a team

Exercise 4:   *To form a team . . .*

This is a fun team-building exercise to be undertaken as soon as a team has formed, and is designed to focus students' attention on what distinguishes a real team from any old cluster of people thrown together. It can help them to recognise in what sense they are not yet a team and what they would need to do to become one. It contains a checklist of suggestions for team-building activities.

Exercise 5:   *To re-form a team . . .*

When teams re-form, for example, after a vacation, to start a second project, and especially after losing or gaining members, they often need to spend a short time re-establishing themselves before they can get down to work effectively. This exercise contains short checklists of questions for students to discuss to help them through what can otherwise be disruptive periods.

Exercise 6:   *How to wreck a team*

The British psyche is often negative and pessimistic rather than positive. If you ask teams to think how they might work effectively this can stop them in their tracks, as they can only think about what might go wrong. This exercise builds on this tendency and involves brainstorming every possible way to guarantee that the team fails and is wrecked by the behaviour of its members. Students find this easy and highly enjoyable! It is then straightforward to turn this negative list into a set of guidelines for effective functioning.

Exercise 7:   *Ground rules*

Exercise 6 is an ideal lead in to Exercise 7, which involves making explicit the ground rules by which each team wants to operate. A team will function much more effectively if there is agreement about such ground rules as those below.

- Aggressive and dominating behaviour is not acceptable.

- All members should turn up to all meetings unless it has been agreed beforehand or unless there are unavoidable circumstances such as illness.

40

- Meetings will start five minutes after the agreed start time and everyone should be there by then.

- Work should be shared around fairly and be seen to be shared fairly.

This exercise helps teams to establish and agree on such ground rules and to keep to them.

Exercise 8: *How teams grow*

This exercise is based on the ideas in Section 3.4 above. It can be very brief and can be undertaken several times at stages as teams develop.

Exercise 9: *How I am in teams*

Students each have their own personal history of being in and working in teams, even if these have been only in the context of sport or hobbies. They have some understanding of how they tend to behave – for example, as "tireless team players" or as prima donnas. If everyone is open about their experiences and what to expect from others this can avoid and defuse otherwise difficult situations and make it more likely that the team can accommodate its individuals and find mutually satisfying ways to operate. The exercise involves a proforma with questions to prompt reflection.

4.4   Sharing and organising the work

Exercise 10: *Team roles*

Sophisticated team leaders perform a range of complementary roles. Student team members largely lack leadership and crucial roles get missed, even such simple ones as time-keeper and note-taker. This exercise involves students allocating such roles to members of the team at the start of a meeting and noticing and discussing how this changed how the meeting went and how the various functions were performed.

Exercise 11: *Who is doing what?*

One of the most important tasks facing a team is dividing up the jobs which need doing and allocating them to appropriate members on an equitable basis. This straightforward exercise involves listing all the tasks which need doing and estimating their size and then allocating them and checking that they are distributed fairly.

Exercise 12: *Time charts*

This exercise follows on from allocating tasks to individuals and requires teams to draw up charts plotting by when various sub-tasks need to be started and finished if everything is to get done by the final deadline. This is particularly important when one task cannot begin until another has been completed or when the tasks allocated to one individual cause an excessive burden at a particular point. The exercise includes a sample chart and leads to the production of the team's own planning chart.

Teamwork development exercises

Exercise 13: *Action planning*

This exercise is designed to help individuals within teams to plan their sub-tasks more thoroughly. Action planning involves the following questions:

- What steps are involved?

- When should they be finished by?

- What will the outcomes look like?

- Who can help you?

- What resources do you need?

- How will you know if you have done it well enough?

The exercise includes a worked example of action planning and takes the team through the steps involved.

4.5   Making meetings work

Exercise 14: *Meetings, bloody meetings*

Despite the popular negative image encapsulated in the John Cleese video *Meetings, Bloody Meetings*, formal meetings have a number of features which are very useful to disorganised student teams. Having a chairperson and an agenda, taking notes about what has been agreed, agreeing when and where to meet next and what the next meeting will deal with – all these are regularly ignored by students with predictable consequences. This exercise explains the basics of formal meetings and gives students the experience of running a meeting in an approved manner so that they can see which of the procedures they wish to adopt in future.

Exercise 15: *Meeting review*

This exercise involves employing a checklist to review what happened in a meeting and can be linked with Exercise 14. The checklist can be used regularly and quickly at the end of meetings to ensure crucial components have not been missed and to improve how the next meeting will go.

Exercise 16: *Chatting by numbers*

Many team meetings resemble purposeless chats. This exercise involves students trying a range of alternatives to unstructured discussion, such as rounds, working alone, pairs, circular interviewing and syndicates. It is best simply to encourage teams to try each of the methods once, perhaps one new method at each meeting, and to take notes on what happened and what methods should be used regularly in the future and under what circumstances.

4.6 Being creative

Exercise 17: *Brainstorming*

Sometimes teams need to stop discussion or work and adopt different patterns of interaction if they are going to be creative and think up solutions to the problems they face. This exercise provides instructions for undertaking a brainstorm so that this creative problem-solving technique can be added to teams' repertoire of working methods.

Exercise 18: *Project pictures*

This exercise is for adventurous teams who would like to explore projective visual methods for envisaging the project they are engaged in. It can help to create a shared vision. This is best undertaken in a classroom with a number of teams present so that groups can see and discuss one another's project pictures and what they signify.

Exercise 19: *How was it for you?*

This is another creative method and involves teams at the start of their work together imagining looking back on the project after it has been completed. It gets out in the open students' hopes and expectations and also throws up many novel ideas which conventional planning would be unlikely to generate.

4.7 Spotting and sorting problems

Exercise 20: *What's going wrong?*

All teams face difficulties at some stage or other, though it isn't always obvious what the problem is about or what is causing it. It is also often painful to raise issues where blame or personalities may be involved. This exercise uses the neutral medium of a checklist containing common problems as a prompt to identifying and raising problems for discussion. Items on the checklist include the following.

What's going wrong?

- We don't listen to one another.
- We keep repeating arguments instead of moving on.
- We constantly interrupt one another.
- We allow assertive members to dominate.
- Some of us don't contribute.
- We don't compromise enough.
- We don't have clear tasks or objectives.
- We are not clear about what has been decided.

The checklist can be used quickly on a number of occasions to see whether action has overcome difficulties or whether they remain to be tackled.

Teamwork development exercises

Exercise 21:   *Who is doing all the talking?*

The most common team problem is simply that some people talk more than is useful while others talk less than would be useful. It is very hard to say this in a team even if it is obvious. This exercise involves employing a simple table which each member uses to estimate the proportion of time each person talks and also what the ideal proportion of contribution would be. This raises many important issues in a way which, though still risky and difficult, is a lot easier than confrontation.

Exercise 22:   *Leading teams*

Teamwork can be used to develop leadership skills, but students are often a little unclear what appropriate forms of leadership actually consist of. The same individuals almost always end up leading, so that most never learn such skills. This exercise encourages students to take turns performing a leadership role in meetings and includes a checklist to review how well this leadership is being undertaken. Again it can be used quickly at the end of any meeting.

Exercise 23:   *Handling problems*

Many of the above exercises will raise students' awareness of what is going on in the team and get out in the open what problems there are. These problems still need to be tackled. In the end someone will have to give feedback to someone else, and that person will have to be able to hear and act on that feedback. A three-stage exercise gives advice and practice on giving and receiving feedback.

4.8   Reporting

Exercise 24:   *How not to give a boring team presentation*

Teams are very often asked to give team presentations at the end of their project and these can be truly dreadful. This exercise involves planning a team presentation based on 14 pieces of advice on how to avoid being really boring.

Exercise 25:   *Team writing*

When teams write joint reports there is often little thought as to how to cooperate in writing. Commonly everyone writes their own bit separately and the whole report is somehow stitched together. Occasionally one person writes the lot. This exercise considers the pros and cons of alternative patterns of cooperative writing and provides planning tools for patterns which involve students performing one of each of the complementary roles of writer, reviewer editor, proofreader and publisher for each of the different components of the report. There are also team reviewing and marking exercises to check the final product before submitting it.

Exercise 26:   *Reporting on teamwork*

This exercise provides a framework for writing a report on teamwork and team skills. It builds on teams having undertaken several of the earlier exercises to develop and review skills and provides a checklist of questions which can be used as headings in a report on teamwork.

4.9   Planning for your next team

Exercise 27:   *Looking back, looking forward*

This exercise is designed to make the most of students' experience of having tackled and completed a team project in order to draw out learning points which can be used to make the next team project more successful, whether it is undertaken in the same team or in a new team on a subsequent course.

5   Bibliography

Belbin, R.M. (1981) *Management Teams: Why They Succeed or Fail*. Oxford: Heinemann.

Bochner, D., Gibbs, G. and Wisker, G. (1995) *Supporting More Students.* Teaching More Students, 6. Oxford: Oxford Centre for Staff Development.

Cuthbert, P. (1994) Self-development groups on a diploma in management studies course. In L. Thorley and R. Gregory, *Using Group-Based Learning in Higher Education*. London: Kogan Page.

Earl, S.E. (1986) Staff and peer assessment: measuring an individual's contribution to group performance. *Assessment and Evaluation in Higher Education*, 11, 60–69.

Falchikov, N. (1988) Self and peer assessment of a group project designed to promote the skills of capability. *Programmed Learning and Educational Technology*, 25, 327–339.

Gibbs, G. (1992a) *Assessing More Students*. (Section 3.4: Assessing Students as Groups). Oxford: Oxford Centre for Staff Development.

Gibbs, G. (1992b) *Discussion with More Students*. Oxford: Oxford Centre for Staff Development.

Gibbs, G. (1994a) *Learning in Teams: A Student Guide*. Oxford: Oxford Centre for Staff Development.

Gibbs, G. (1994b) *Learning in Teams: A Student Manual*. Oxford: Oxford Centre for Staff Development.

Goldfinch, J. and Raeside, R. (1990) Development of a peer assessment technique for obtaining individual marks on a group project. *Assessment and Evaluation in Higher Education*, 15/3, 210–231.

Hartley, J. and Bahra, H. (1992) Study networks: support mechanisms for large groups of part time students. In G. Gibbs and A. Jenkins (eds), *Teaching Large Classes*. London: Kogan Page.

Hastings, C., Bixby, P. and Chandhry-Lawton, R. (1986) *Superteams*. London: Fontana.

Jaques, D. (1991) *Learning in Groups*. London: Kogan Page.

Jenkins, A. and Pepper, D. (1988) *Enhancing Employability and Educational Experience: a Manual on Teaching Communication and Groupwork Skills in Higher Education*, Paper 27. Birmingham: Standing Conference on Educational Development.

Larson, C. and La Fasto, F. (1989) *Team Work*. London: Sage.

Lejk, M. (1994) Team assessment, win or lose. *The New Academic*, Summer, 10–11.

Pedler, M. (1986) Development within the organisation: experiences with management self-development groups. *Management Education and Development*, 17, 1.

Platt, S. (1988) *Teams: A Game to Develop Group Skills*. Aldershot: Gower.

Storey, R. (1989) *Team Building: A Manual for Leaders and Trainers*. London: BACIE.

Thorley, L. and Gregory, R. (1994) *Using Group-Based Learning in Higher Education*. London: Kogan Page.

Topping, K. (1988) *The Peer Tutoring Handbook: Promoting Cooperative Learning.* Beckenham: Croom Helm.

Usher, J.R. (1990) Development of a staff and peer assessment scheme for groupwork in mathematical modelling. *Teaching Mathematics and its Applications,* 9, 1–5.

Verran, J. (1993) Group projects in biological science. *The New Academic,* 2/2, 9–11.

Woodcock, M. (1989) *Team Development Manual.* Aldershot: Gower.

Woodcock, M. (1989) *50 Activities of Teambuilding.* Aldershot: Gower.

Other publications available from the Oxford Centre for Staff Development

COURSE DESIGN FOR RESOURCE BASED LEARNING

Course Design for Resource Based Learning in Social Science
Course Design for Resource Based Learning in Education
Course Design for Resource Based Learning in Technology
Course Design for Resource Based Learning in Accountancy
Course Design for Resource Based Learning in Built Environment
Course Design for Resource Based Learning in Art and Design
Course Design for Resource Based Learning in Business
Course Design for Resource Based Learning in Humanities
Course Design for Resource Based Learning in Science
Institutional Support for Resource Based Learning

LEARNING IN TEAMS

Learning in Teams: A Student Guide
Learning in Teams: A Student Manual
Learning in Teams: A Tutor Guide

DEVELOPING WRITING SERIES

Essential Writing Skills
Using Data
Writing Reports
Scientific & Technical Writing
Essay Writing
Tutor Manual

DEVELOPING STUDENTS' TRANSFERABLE SKILLS

STRATEGIES FOR DIVERSIFYING ASSESSMENT

BEING AN EFFECTIVE ACADEMIC

IMPROVING STUDENT LEARNING – THEORY AND PRACTICE

IMPROVING STUDENT LEARNING – THROUGH ASSESSMENT AND
EVALUATION

ASSESSING STUDENT CENTRE COURSES